Housewarming Parties

poems

Jaci Schreckengost

Lunar Lit Press

Lunar Lit Press
www.lunarlitpress.com

ISBN-13: 979-8-9940300-0-4 (paperback)
ISBN-13: 979-8-9940300-1-1 (ebook)

Cover design by Connor Bryan
Designed and typeset by Connor Bryan in Goudy Old
Style 12/18

Printed in the United States of America

"...And what if, after everything you've waited through, something beautiful and worthwhile still awaits you?"

— Morgan Harper Nichols

Contents

They Must Go

After Christina Forrer's Woman (with eyes open)

A feeling of solitude hits

as she lies on her bedroom

floor. She catches her

reflection in the closet door mirror,

stares gravely at the woman

looking back at her. She

is wondering how to

unravel herself. How to

pull on a loose end

a little too hard.

But she's afraid unraveling

herself won't be enough —

these thoughts, the feeling

of solitude will still exist,

woven into the very

fibers she is made of.

She jumps up, her feet

flat on the floor, ready to run;

ready to chase after a

version of her that

does not feel the need

to rip herself apart.

Self-Portrait as a Spare Room

There is so much space.

Instead of using it well,

I am full of unpacked

boxes, unorganized

books, pictures I

never hung on the

walls. Visitors tell me

there is so much potential.

No One Is Coming to Save You

Thank God.

I do not want

someone to try

and save me only

to figure out that I was

really the wreckage all along.

The Yarn of the Universe

She pulls and pulls,

trying, desperately,

to unravel herself.

Once she got to

the tip of her toes,

she thought it

was the end.

But she just needed the

thread, loose and free,

to create something new.

Boxes

The first time, I'm sure,

I destroyed the box by

accident.

I don't remember it —

too many ruined

boxes to count since

that first one —

but my guess is that

I took too deep of

a breath, expanded

on the exhale, and

the sides gave way.

So I shrunk myself

and held my breath

in the next box, nearly

letting myself suffocate

within the walls until I

outstretched my arms,

broke through the tape

I'd placed myself.

Rinse and repeat, I'd

squeeze myself into

a new box, stick new

labels on the side,

hoping they'd make

it feel more welcoming

but I always ended up

breathing as shallowly

as possible, praying

this would be the time

the box would

finally hold its shape.

Each time, I climbed in,

taking breaths that barely

gave me enough oxygen

to survive, pretending that

each shallow exhale didn't

come with a question:

What happens next?

In Hot Water

Too little, too late,

I realized the water

was boiling. It still

took even longer

to realize this meant

I was boiling, too.

Did I climb in? Or did

someone toss me?

Maybe it doesn't

matter how I got

here. But that I

jump out, turn

off the burner,

put the pan

in the sink,

and go on

with my

life.

Human Nature

I want to bottle the sunrise,

and pour it over my hands.

I'll lather them with the soap

I made out of the mountains.

On the best days, I want to

bottle up the entire ocean in

a Mason jar and examine it

closely. I want to sit it on my

bookshelf and stare into

the deep blue unknown

because I think it will

somehow help me

understand myself.

I want to encapsulate the

infinite — human nature, I

suppose — and control it,

waste it on myself.

Human nature, indeed.

Alchemy in Skagit Valley

I'm standing in the woods

when a version of myself,

one I hadn't even known

was different than the one

before, leaves. She walks

down the gravel road and

I find myself chasing after

her, trying to call her name,

but I don't even know it.

I cannot catch up, cannot

force a semblance of who

I used to be. I am left standing

in the middle of the trees,

forced to ask why I was

so desperate to remain

someone I didn't

even acknowledge until

it was too late. The silence urges

me to let the newness breathe,

and bask in the alchemized me.

I Ask the Elements If I'll Be Alright

There were days

I was willing

to freeze if

it meant the

snow accepted me.

Days I was

willing to drown

if it meant

the waves loved

me. Days I

was willing to

burn if I

would find myself

in the fire,

bury myself if

it meant the

soil would tell

me why I'm

here but they

always shook me

out and tossed

me back into

the world and

onto my feet.

I Met My Younger Self for Coffee

After Jennae Cecelia

I met her at the Starbucks on campus. I watched

as she contemplated what to order, embarrassed

by what she really wanted. She didn't know what to
do

with her hands, her heart, any part of herself.

She showed up after breaking up with her boyfriend

and is trying to find the acceptable balance

between sadness and relief, focused on trying to be

what she thinks everyone else wants her to be —

instead of just being whatever the fuck she is.

I slide my right hand over my left to cover my rings.

She doesn't believe in this kind of love yet.

She tells me she doesn't know what's next and I

try to assure her this really is the first day of the rest of her life. She rolls her eyes before I finish the sentence and I laugh because I should have seen that coming. I stop trying to convince her that she will look back on this day as a new beginning, and just let her find out for herself.

When I Think of Home, I Think Of

sitting at the wooden table in the kitchen at our house in West Virginia / watching the sun shine in just right / the loft where I slept when we were in Louisiana / I don't even remember the name of the town / staring into pure darkness at sea in the middle of the night / wondering why this feels so much like home / evenings watching Desperate Housewives with my mom / the three year old me who started searching for home as soon as she realized she didn't know where it was / kicking the truck into reverse with her foot in case we passed it already / walking in Kansas with my dad / my favorite park in Melbourne / the books I've read that have met me exactly where I was / airport carpet / sobbing outside a cabin in Washington / the first night at the house in Florida / passing by cities on a solo train trip / getting the keys to the place in Pooler on our anniversary / a now-defunct courthouse / a wooden desk in a classroom in Savannah / our spot under a tree in Orlando / all the times I prayed home would click into place one day / but instead, it just kept moving / feeling like a cat who can never catch the little red laser, secretly getting high from the rush of the chase / everything and nothing, all at once

A Young Libra Trying to Find Herself

is a painful thing for everyone

to witness — some bizarre

combination of stubborn and

unaware. When her searches

turn up unsuccessful, she makes

her way home, frustrated and furious,

until she opens the door to find

her reflection staring back at her.

"I've been looking for you everywhere."

I know, the reflection will

roll her eyes and say.

I was with you the whole time.

Apple Pie Moonshine

I blink and the plane is landing.

We rush to your house from the

airport to drink apple pie moonshine

out of Mason jars in your living room.

I blink and I do not realize that it's

weird you've been standing across

the room from me most of the night.

I blink and I'm playing drinking

games with people I do not know.

The few I do know are telling

me secrets you haven't told me yet.

I blink and I wake up between

the mattress and the wall, half

wanting to stay and half wanting

to take the next flight out.

I blink and I wake up between the

two people I've always been: the

person who called this place home

in the first draft and the person who

took it out while revising.

Places I've Stashed Pieces of Myself

After Michelle Awad

I started picking parts

of myself apart at a

young age and storing

them wherever I found

room, thinking each

piece I left somewhere

else would mean that

I'd take up less space.

So I left a pinch of my

excitement in the garden

where I rode a four-wheeler

and I left a handful of my

seven-year-old dance moves

in the refrigerated section

at the Walmart in Spencer

and I left too much joy behind

bushes on a college campus

and I left an arm and a leg's

worth of laughter in an office

the first time a manager told

me I was too loud and I left

my voice in my glovebox,

only breaking it out when I

was alone, and now, I am

almost thankful I left all

these things years ago, because

now I get to go collect them.

Places I've Found Pieces of Myself

After Michelle Awad

Map in hand, backpack in tow,

every now and then I go

full Hobbit on a journey to

find a piece of myself I'd

once stashed away.

I've rummaged through

campus trash cans to find

my confidence, years after

I dumped it there.

I scoured a parking lot in

Charleston to find the little girl,

still with her hands on her hips,

who said, "I'll have my own money,"

when someone told her she'd

better marry rich.

I stashed a bit of my certainty

in the rose garden at Forsyth

but remembered to take a detour

and pick it up before we left town.

One day, maybe, I'll stop

leaving myself behind at all.

Have I Been Here Before?

And on the rarest occasions,

I've found old pieces

of myself in places I was

visiting for the first time.

I learned there's a path directly into my soul

that exists in the woods in Skagit Valley

and the live oaks in Savannah told

me they'd known me for ages,

whispered the secrets I'd been

holding close to my chest to prove it,

forcing me to acknowledge that

this world is nothing new and

even when I'm afraid this is the

end of my journey, I am really

just getting started.

So Tell Me About Yourself

My answer to this question changes monthly, weekly, daily / but no matter the variation, the first thing I'll tell you is that I'm a writer / it's the one identity I will bear hug and white-knuckle to my deathbed / and I'm so tired of answering this question, mostly because I will either say too much or too little / and either way, people seem to be disappointed / and speaking of bears, most days I will tell you 'of course I'd pick the bear' / the others, I will tell you that I am the bear / and I really believe it, too, while I'm standing in my office doing my Rebecca Welton power pose / and I will tell you that otters hold hands while they nap so they don't lose each other / and I will tear up while I say it, even for the thousandth time / and I *can* be the bear and the woman who cries about otters at the same time / and I believe that butterfly just crossed my backyard especially for me / and I found a note in my phone that says 'I am like a light show in an airport' / and by that, I'm sure I meant *extra* / but you can take it however you'd like / and my laugh echoes through hotels, walls, universes / people tell me that's how they found me / like I said, probably more than you wanted to know

When My Niece Asks if the Moon Is Going to Fall

My niece asks if the moon is going to fall

and I stand silently because I really

don't know what to say.

I see why she asked — the full moon

feels closer than normal, like it might

be trying to tell us something before it goes away.

Part of me wants to wrap her in a hug

and tell her of course not,

but I don't know that life will go that way.

Instead, I say nothing, and she moves on

before I have a good answer. She forgets

she even asked, but I hold the memory like a bouquet.

Months later, when I realize she was asking

not out of fear but out of moonstruck curiosity,

I want to rattle off a million questions her way.

If she ever asks again,

I will tell her I don't know,

but I'll lift her up if she wants to hear what it has to
say.

An Ode to the People Who Have Told Me My Dreams Are Unrealistic

After Turbulence II by Dave Pollot

I always told them I would rip

the grey skies open, if I needed to,

but they still stood and stared in dismay

as I reached up above the horizon,

found the seam, and pulled.

I know — isn't it incredible?

Being Alive Is a Special Occasion

If we are

honest, the special

occasions

are just days

we admit that none of this

will last forever.

Cheers

After Mindy Nettifee

Every so often,

I grab the

champagne glasses

from the highest

cabinet and I toast

the girl who couldn't

do cartwheels and

hated having her hair

curled. I toast the girl

who took the steps

and fell flat on her

face. I used to only

toast her because

she stood back up.

Now, I toast her for

all of it. I open my

eyes and see the

woman looking back

at me in the mirror.

I toast her.

I have a million reasons why,

but I finally know

I don't need one.

A Continuous Reinvention

I've spent a lifetime trying

to put myself into words,

trying to understand where

I landed, trying to balance

feeling like I was too much

for everyone else and never

enough for myself, and,

for right now at least —

I've decided I'm like one of

those theme park rides that

is a series of interconnected

circles, whipping around in a

figure eight, always on the move,

something new every few seconds.

Some turns feel like close calls, but they

never really crash into one another.

Some people cringe when they

look at it — others say it's their favorite.

And just when I think I need

to pick a lane or just suck it

up and be a one-trick pony or a

one-track amusement park ride,

Morgan Harper Nichols reminds

me that I am free to begin

again and I take that to mean

that I am free to begin

again and again and again.

A Funeral for the Living

I threw a funeral for

a version of myself

who left us unexpectedly.

Many had come and gone

before, but this time felt

more formal, like we were

really losing someone worth mourning,

so I dressed in black —

somehow both a grieving

attendee and the deceased.

When I stepped up to the coffin,

I realized the bags under her eyes

were deep and weary. Her neck

tired from looking down. Her mind

slowed nearly to a halt in the days

before she went. If I pried open

her eyelids, those wide, once-glassy

windows into her soul would tell me

she was swallowing strings with gum

attached at the end, trying to reach

deep inside her to fish out

the spark she knew was there.

They said it was untimely,

when we choked on that string.

But I knew it was right.

But the next time one of us moves on,

I'm wearing sequins and

hiring a DJ instead of buying a casket.

Housewarming Parties

I'm starting the tradition of

throwing a housewarming party

for every new version of myself.

As soon as I feel the slightest hint of returning,

I begin planning the details, confirming

the color of the napkins I'll use

before I even mark the date on the calendar.

Later, I'll write the invites,

seal the envelopes with delight,

and take a deep breath

when all that's left on the table is my hope.

I'll use my excitement to blow up the balloons,

my dreams to fill the platters,

my refreshed heart to open the door

and welcome in my loved ones.

But I know the party doesn't

start until I'm singing

Jake Wesley Rogers and

Florence and the Machine with

such gusto that the cars passing by

the party have to hear, at least a little.

I hope they start to sing along.

Since We're Throwing Things

Since we're throwing things, I want you to

toss your rules out the window and

see what happens if you dance

on top of the coffee

table. Did the world

come to an end?

Either way,

carry

on.

I Do Not Want to Celebrate Alone

When I say this, I want you to know

that I will if I have to —

I will stand alone

in a dark kitchen

with a candle in the

middle of a cookie cake,

breaking off

the pieces with the

most icing until

my teeth are dyed

more colors than

I care to count

when I smile at myself

in the mirror.

But I'd rather

look over

to see you

celebrating, too.

I want you to throw

a housewarming party

for every new version

of yourself, even

if you're not sure she's

here to stay — don't

we deserve to be

celebrated anyway?

Acknowledgments

First, thank you to Connor for creating Moonstruck Market and Lunar Lit Press — and for inviting me to be a part of it through this publication. Some pieces in this collection date back five years, and I'm so thankful to see them find a home.

I'd also like to acknowledge the artists who inspired any of the work in this collection, including Michelle Awad, Jennae Cecelia, Christina Forrer, Morgan Harper Nichols, Mindy Nettifee, and Dave Pollot. Thank you all for sharing your work with the world.

Of course, a huge thank you to Alex, my parents, Jeff and Susie, my family, all of my bonus parents, and my friends for supporting me through this. Regardless of whether you knew I was working on it or not, you were supporting me along the way, and I am grateful. I don't know what I did to deserve such wonderful people in my life.

About the Author

Jaci Schreckengost is a freelance writer, marketer, and multifaceted creative based in Melbourne, Florida. She has spent more than 8 years in content, digital, and social media marketing, helping brands across industries find their voices and effectively tell their stories. Her work has appeared in several print and online publications including *Reverie Magazine* and *Stone Circle Review*. She holds an MFA in writing from the Savannah College of Art and Design. When she's not writing, she loves reading, traveling, and spending time with her husband and their dog.

Find out more about Jaci online at jacischreckengost.com and on Instagram at @schreckengostcreative.

www.ingramcontent.com/pod-product-compliance
Lightning Source LLC
Chambersburg PA
CBHW051648120626
46551CB00015B/2273